SPEAK
"FACE" BOOK?!

Rob Key

SPEAK
"FACE"BOOK?!

A Fun and Intriguing Way
To Spice Up Your Facebook Posts

TATE PUBLISHING
AND ENTERPRISES, LLC

Speak "Face"book?!
Copyright © 2014 by Rob Key. All rights reserved.

No part of this publication may be reproduced, stored in a retrieval system or transmitted in any way by any means, electronic, mechanical, photocopy, recording or otherwise without the prior permission of the author except as provided by USA copyright law.

This book is designed to provide accurate and authoritative information with regard to the subject matter covered. This information is given with the understanding that neither the author nor Tate Publishing, LLC is engaged in rendering legal, professional advice. Since the details of your situation are fact dependent, you should additionally seek the services of a competent professional.

The opinions expressed by the author are not necessarily those of Tate Publishing, LLC.

Published by Tate Publishing & Enterprises, LLC
127 E. Trade Center Terrace | Mustang, Oklahoma 73064 USA
1.888.361.9473 | www.tatepublishing.com

Tate Publishing is committed to excellence in the publishing industry. The company reflects the philosophy established by the founders, based on Psalm 68:11,
"The Lord gave the word and great was the company of those who published it."

Book design copyright © 2014 by Tate Publishing, LLC. All rights reserved.
Cover design by Gian Philipp Rufin
Interior design by Jimmy Sevilleno

Published in the United States of America

ISBN: 978-1-63418-090-0
1. Self-Help / Communication & Social Skills
2. Language Arts & Disciplines / Linguistics / Sociolinguistics
14.10.07

CONTENTS

Introduction 7
"Face"Starters 9
"Face"A–D 35
"Face"E–I 79
"Face"J–P 117
"Face"Q–S 155
"Face"T–Z 195

INTRODUCTION

Facebook is the modern day phenomena that enables you to share your everyday life experiences and thoughts with your family and friends by avenues such as pictures and written posts through your computer, smartphone, or tablet. You can share big news like having a baby or you can share that you just made the perfect cup of coffee. You can post pictures from your vacation or you can post a *selfie*. So would it not be cool to have some universal terms that anyone, young or old, could use while on Facebook? Why not have a word that everyone could instantly recognize as being significant in a post? Well, what you will find in this book is an extensive list of words that you can use to punctuate and give a new vibe to your updating. Because these words are Facebook-specific, all of them have "Face" in them. Some are self-explanatory, such as "*Face*"*food*, which basically means "all things food." Other words may require you to think some, like "*Face*"*down* or "*Face*"*bomb*, since their meaning can be ambiguous. Still others would make you think really hard, like "*Face*"*guaced*, the meaning of which you will discover in the pages to come!

So have fun with this!

"FACE" STARTERS

"FACE"LIFT

To be encouraged by someone's comment on your Facebook page or to give encouragement to someone by giving a positive comment on their update or wall.

How to use it:

"Thanks for the *'Face'lift* today, everyone! Your birthday wishes are much appreciated!"

"FACE"IAL

A new profile picture.

How to use it:

"Greetings, family and friends! Check out my '*Face'ial*! Took the pic at my niece's wedding!"

"FACE"CHECK

Reading through people's posts on the News Feed.

How to use it:

"I spent my entire coffee break doing a '*Face*'check. Now I'm really inspired to finish the day strong!"

SPEAK "FACE"BOOK?!

"FACE"SKIZZY

A warm and fuzzy status update or comment.

How to use it:

"What a great '*Face'skizzy*! You really know how to make me feel good!"

"FACE" GUARD

Not becoming friends with everyone who requests it.

How to use it:

"I do some *'Face'guarding* every once in a while—not sure I want to get updates on everyone whom I meet."

"FACE"HOG

A friend who seems to be taking up way too much of your News Feed.

How to use it:

"I barely get a chance to catch up on all my friends' posts because someone (to remain anonymous) is a *'Face'hog*! I don't need an update on your update all the time!"

"FACE"HOUND

Someone who tries to be friends with as many people as possible—could be positive or negative.

How to use it:

"My brother has so many friends on Facebook that he is turning into a *'Face'hound*! I doubt he even really knows half of them."

SPEAK "FACE"BOOK?!

"FACE"DATE

To go on a date or to date a Facebook friend.

How to use it:

"Guess what, peeps? I'm going on a *'Face'date* tonight! Looking forward to dining by the beach on this lovely evening!"

ROB KEY

"FACE"VITE

Using the social network to invite your friends to an event.

How to use it:

"Hey, everyone! Here's your special *'Face'vite* to my sister's baby shower. Save the date and time. Other details to come soon. You don't want to miss it!"

SPEAK "FACE"BOOK?!

"FACE"PUNCH

A friendly jab at you or at a friend's post on Facebook.

How to use it:

"Yes, I got a lot of '*Face'punches* about my last status update, but they were all well deserved on my part!"

"FACE"BOMB

Big news in your status update.

How to use it:

"*Face'bomb* alert! Just found out that we are pregnant! Baby is due in November!"

"FACE"CRINGE

It's what you get when you read a status update that makes you feel very uncomfortable—way too much personal information given.

How to use it:

"Steve, your post gave me a *'Face'cringe*! We really did not need to know the details of your grandmother's colostomy."

"FACE" MAGNET

A person who is able to attract a lot of friends to their social networking site.

How to use it:

"My friend Samantha is a *'Face'magnet*! She has so many friends that I can't keep up with her. Everyone she meets requests to be friends with her!"

"FACE"PLANT

Happens when you posted something stupid on Facebook.

How to use it:

"Wow, did I ever just do a *'Face'plant* with that last update! I guess I wasn't thinking straight and posted without reading the whole thing first."

ROB KEY

"FACE"YOKED

An extremely strong or powerful update, picture, or comment.

How to use it:

"Man, that picture is '*Face'yoked*! You really motivated me to begin that fitness plan! I have been procrastinating for years."

SPEAK "FACE"BOOK?!

"FACE"WALLY

The game of "Where am I?" using pictures and clues.

How to use it:

"*Face'Wally* time! Can anyone guess where I am sitting right now? It's hard to believe that I even had access to this place."

"FACE" CARPED

You got suckered or fooled by a friend on Facebook!

How to use it:

"Wow! You had me hook, line, and sinker on that one! It never entered my mind that you *'Face'carped* me!"

SPEAK "FACE"BOOK?!

"FACE"SPECTIVE

Your current perspective.

How to use it:

"My *Face'spective* today after lunch… taking in this band who was playing in the plaza…so beautiful!"

"FACE"FLART

A brainfart or a brainlapse. Either way you accidentally posted a wrong picture.

How to use it:

"Sorry, folks! I just had a *'Face'flart*! This is the correct picture of us on our anniversary…not the one of the dude in the spandex!"

"FACE"SIGHTING

Sightings of well-known people.

How to use it:

"I didn't expect to have this *'Face'sighting* at breakfast, but the mayor came in and sat at the table right next to ours. I guess he likes a good omelet to start the day like I do!"

"FACE" FRAZZED

Venting or showing frustration about something.

How to use it:

"Ok, I'm a little *'Face'frazzed* right now. I just need to get my feelings out in the open. Why do we need to keep hearing about that all the time? It was old news last year!"

SPEAK "FACE"BOOK?!

"FACE"POSTERED

A picture that shows you getting the better of someone.

How to use it:

"Just *'Face'postered* my friend. He had no clue I was coming around the corner!"

ROB KEY

"FACE" FRECKLE

A cute post or picture.

How to use it:

"Here's a *'Face'freckle* for your day! I was at a dairy farm earlier today, and I snapped this cool pic!"

SPEAK "FACE"BOOK?!

"FACE"PAG

Being passive aggressive in your posts.

How to use it:

"What's up with being a *'Face'pagger* all of a sudden? Just tell us what you really want. We can help you out, bro!"

"FACE" JAM

A "selfie" with more than one person in it all crammed together.

How to use it:

"On the elevator going up to the sky suites we took this lovely 'Face'jam. Everyone was so pumped to see the view!"

"FACE" A–D

"FACE"ABLE

A person who is new to Facebook and can now use it correctly.

How to use it:

"Hey, I know I'm late for the party, but I am now finally '*Face'able*! Glad to be so connected to all my family and friends!"

SPEAK "FACE"BOOK?!

"FACE"ALERT

A very important message to your friends on Facebook—good or bad.

How to use it:

"*Face'alert*! Hey, Panther Soccer fans, I just heard that the soccer game has been postponed due to lightning in the area. I will keep you updated if I hear anything new. Thanks!"

"FACE"ALICIOUS

A description of someone who posted a very attractive picture of themselves.

How to use it:

"You look so *'Face'alicious* in your new pic! Where did you get your new hairstyle?"

SPEAK "FACE"BOOK?!

"FACE"AMPED

A post that is stronger than normal.

How to use it:

"Dude, you are '*Face'amped*! I love it when you post with such passion!"

"FACE" ART

A profile picture that is artfully put together. Definitely some thought was put into how it will appear.

How to use it:

"Great *'Face'art* in your new picture! Love, love, love the way the whole family looks!"

"FACE"BABE

Your special someone.

How to use it:

"Hey, '*Face'babe*, wanna go out tonight? I'm thinking we should check out that new movie and then grab some dessert!"

"FACE"BABY

One that whines too much in their updates.

How to use it:

"Yo, dude, stop being a '*Face'baby* in your posts. Some positivity would help in your situation. Come on, man!"

SPEAK "FACE"BOOK?!

"FACE"BIKERS

A biking club of friends.

How to use it:

"Calling all fellow '*Face'bikers*! Plan to do the mountain loop this Saturday at 7:00 a.m. Meet at Mike's Bike Shop."

"FACE"BLAH

Saying basically nothing in your post. An empty update.

How to use it:

"I know that previous post was a *Face'blah*. I just had nothing new going on, but I wanted everyone to know that I am still alive and kicking."

SPEAK "FACE"BOOK?!

"FACE"BLAST

A quick significant note to all your friends.

How to use it:

"*'Face'blast*! We got first place at the tourney!"

"FACE"BLESSED

Feeling fortunate for having such a great group of friends in your social network.

How to use it:

"I am so '*Face'blessed*! I have felt so much love from you all during my time in the hospital! Can't wait to finally get back to full strength."

SPEAK "FACE"BOOK?!

"FACE"BLITZ

Using your social network to inform of a specific event.

How to use it:

"*Face'blitz* all your friends about the free concert in the park coming up in May. Sounds like there should be a good number of local bands playing."

"FACE"BLOB

A very long and boring update.

How to use it:

"Well, that was a '*Face'blob*. Sorry for such a time-consuming and pointless post!"

"FACE"BLOCK

Blocking a person to restrict them from starting conversations, adding you as friend, or seeing posts from your timeline.

How to use it:

"Remember that guy from senior high who was stalking me? I '*Face*'blocked him before he could even think of adding me as a friend."

ROB KEY

"FACE"BOMB

Big news in your status update.

How to use it:

"*Face'bomb* alert! Just found out that we are pregnant! Baby is due in November!"

"FACE"BONE

It's how you ask for help.

How to use it:

"Will someone throw me a *'Face'bone* please? I need some major help figuring out this puzzle. It's been on my mind for the better part of the day!"

"FACE"BOUNCED

Unfriended someone.

How to use it:

"I got '*Face'bounced* by one of my friends yesterday. What's up with that? I suppose they didn't like some of my posts."

"FACE"BROS

A group of your male friends on Facebook or all your male friends on Facebook.

How to use it:

"Got together with some of my *'Face'bros* for lunch today! Had a great time connecting with those guys again; been too long since we've done that!"

"FACE"BURN

You got insulted by one of your friends on Facebook.

How to use it:

"Didn't realize that by liking one of my friend's posts, I was going to get *'Face'burned* by a different friend. Guess they didn't appreciate where I came from."

"FACE"BUY

The purchase of something found through Facebook.

How to use it:

"Thanks, Allison, for pointing me to that great deal! That was such a fabulous *'Face'buy*! Now I won't need to shop for those until next year."

"FACE"BUZZ

The latest, most popular news going around.

How to use it:

"Hey, friends, what's up with this latest *'Face'buzz*? I am quite sure that's not going to happen, but I have been wrong before. Unbelievable!"

"FACE" CARD

A funny friend on Facebook.

How to use it:

"Tyler, my man, you are such a '*Face'card*! Every time you post something, I can't wait to read it because it's usually very entertaining!"

"FACE"CARPED

You got suckered or tricked by a friend on Facebook!

How to use it:

"Wow! You had me hook, line, and sinker on that one! It never entered my mind that you 'Face'carped me!"

SPEAK "FACE"BOOK?!

"FACE"CHECK

Reading through people's posts on the News Feed.

How to use it:

"I spent my entire coffee break doing a '*Face*'check. Now I'm really inspired to finish the day strong!"

"FACE"CHIEF

The one you recognize as the biggest leader of your friends.

How to use it:

"You are definitely the '*Face'chief* among all my friends. You know just the right things to say to get me going! Thank you!"

"FACE"CHOKE

Happens when you post something that was not correct.

How to use it:

"I '*Face'choked* big time on that update! We have been married for nineteen years, not sixteen. Yes, I know I'm in big trouble over that one. Better treat her like the princess that she is tonight!"

"FACE"CLUB

Any group that you communicate with via Facebook.

How to use it:

"Tonight for '*Face'club*, we are going to meet at Andre's house. Be there no later than 7:00, and make sure you bring a snack to share. Rock on!"

SPEAK "FACE"BOOK?!

"FACE"CLUES

Profile information to help identify a potential friend.

How to use it:

> "I finally figured out the right match for you once I looked closer at the *'Face'clues*. I didn't realize there were that many people with your exact name! Some of the pictures weren't helpful either. I am overly thankful I found you!"

"FACE" CONSTRICTOR

Someone who takes the fun out of Facebook.

How to use it:

"Seriously, stop being such a *'Face'constrictor*! You are being way too serious all the time. I'm getting tired of seeing your posts with all your junk."

"FACE"COVER

It's what you have on when you don't disclose pertinent profile information, either on purpose or by accident. Thus, it makes it harder for potential friends to find you.

How to use it:

"Cassie, I wasn't sure that was you with that '*Face'cover* on. Glad we are able to connect finally. I could not remember what state you live in now, and you had nothing about what school you went to. Anyway, let's catch up soon!"

"FACE"CRED

It's what you have when you are well respected by your friends.

How to use it:

"Kaleysha has such good *'Face'cred*. Her updates are so well put together and are definitely not obnoxious. I always look forward to hearing from her!"

"FACE" CREME

It's what you need after a horrible post to help soothe yourself.

How to use it:

"Dude, you need some serious '*Face'creme* after that flaky post! That was awkward!"

"FACE" CREW

Your Facebook friends.

How to use it:

"Attention, *'Face'crew*! I am in need of some big-time help this weekend as we are moving to our new house. Anyone feeling ambitious? Let's meet at our current house at 8:00 a.m., Saturday, if you can. There will be plenty of food and beverages!"

SPEAK "FACE"BOOK?!

"FACE"CRINGE

It's what you get when you read a status update that makes you feel very uncomfortable—way too much personal information given.

How to use it:

"Steve, your post gave me a '*Face'cringe*! We really did not need to know the details of your grandmother's colostomy. Next time spare me the details!"

"FACE"CRUSH

You adore someone romantically or in a friendly manner.

How to use it:

"I must have a *'Face'crush* on you, man! I look forward to reading your posts more than anyone else! You've got that passion that I want!"

SPEAK "FACE"BOOK?!

"FACE"DATE

To go on a date or to date a Facebook friend.

How to use it:

"Guess what, peeps? I'm going on a '*Face'date* tonight! Looking forward to dining by the beach on this lovely evening!"

"FACE" DAY

Your birthday!

How to use it:

"It's your *'Face'day*! Time to celebrate, sister! Happy birthday, my friend!"

SPEAK "FACE"BOOK?!

"FACE"DODGE

Avoiding contact with a current or potential friend.

How to use it:

"A couple of friends from my past who were bad influences on me tried to friend me, but for now I'm going to '*Face'dodge* them. Maybe in time I will get back in contact with them but right now, it feels too soon."

"FACE"DOS

Appropriate ways to use Facebook.

How to use it:

"Hey, Dylan! Letting your friends know of significant events in your life is definitely one of the '*Face'dos* of Facebook. It's not bragging, so don't be so concerned."

SPEAK "FACE"BOOK?!

"FACE"DON'TS

Inappropriate ways to use Facebook.

How to use it:

"One of my '*Face'don'ts* is to not post when I'm leaving town and when I'll be back. I don't want anyone to get any crazy ideas!"

"FACE"DOWN

A way to tell your friends you will not be updating/using Facebook for a few days.

How to use it:

"I'm going *'Face'down* for the rest of the week. If you need to contact me then please give me a call on my cell."

"FACE"DROP

Telling your friends about a well-known person who is your friend.

How to use it:

"I know I'm about to '*Face'drop*, but the lead actor from this season's number one show just became one of my friends. How cool is that?"

"FACE" E-I

"FACE"ETIQUETTE

A proper and prudent use of Facebook.

How to use it:

"She has such good '*Face'etiquette*! She always has something brilliant to say and never puts anyone down. She is definitely a must-read!"

SPEAK "FACE"BOOK?!

"FACE" EXPOSED

When someone's posts show a different side of them other than the side you know.

How to use it:

"I believe I got an eye-opener by reading through one of my friend's pages. Facebook definitely '*Face'exposed* them."

"FACE"FAIL

A lame update.

How to use it:

"Dude, that was a 'F*ace'fail*! You must have been in a hurry because that post was pitiful."

SPEAK "FACE"BOOK?!

"FACE"FAM

Can refer literally to your family on Facebook or to all your friends on Facebook.

How to use it:

"Hey, *'Face'fam*! I received tremendous news today—I got the job!"

"FACE" FIRST

Something you have seen for the first time on Facebook.

How to use it:

"Well, that was a *'Face'first*! Didn't think my grandma would ever join the Facebook nation, but I guess she is savvier than I think! You go, Grandma!"

SPEAK "FACE"BOOK?!

"FACE"FIT

Your Facebook page is in good shape (it looks great).

How to use it:

"I feel like I am '*Face'fit* now; I have my homepage just the way I like it!"

"FACE"FLART

A brainfart or a brainlapse. Either way you accidentally posted a wrong picture.

How to use it:

"Sorry, folks! I just had a *'Face'flart*! This is the correct picture of us on our anniversary…not the one of the dude in the spandex!"

"FACE"FLEX

Bragging a little.

How to use it:

"Got some *'Face'flex* for you...my daughter just got straight A's on her report card this semester. So proud of her!"

"FACE"FLUENT

One who knows and uses Facebook proficiently.

How to use it:

"Remember, Wanda, the more you use Facebook, the more '*Face'fluent* you'll become. So just start playing around with it. You'll be an expert in no time!"

"FACE"FOE

Not a friend *yet* on Facebook.

How to use it:

"Yeah, it's hard to believe we used to be '*Face'foes*, but now I really enjoy getting your updates. You have become such a great friend!"

"FACE"FOOD

All things food (recipes, restaurant recommendations, etc.).

How to use it:

"I have a '*Face'food* question: Does anyone have a yummy recipe for an organic dessert that includes chocolate? My husband really wants to start making more healthy choices, so I thought I would help him out."

SPEAK "FACE"BOOK?!

"FACE"FRAZZED

Venting or showing frustration about something.

How to use it:

"Okay, I'm a little *'Face'frazzed* right now. I just need to get my feelings out in the open. Why do we need to keep hearing about that all the time? It was old news last year!"

"FACE" FRECKLE

A cute post or picture.

How to use it:

"Here's a '*Face'freckle* for your day! I was at a dairy farm earlier today and I snapped this cool pic!"

SPEAK "FACE"BOOK?!

"FACE"FREE

A profile picture without your face.

How to use it:

"I decided to change my profile pic to a *'Face'free* picture since the sunset was so awesome tonight. Good night, all!"

"FACE" FRIDAY

The day when you let your friends know of your weekend plans and of any possible way to connect with them.

How to use it:

"Hello, Friends! It's '*Face*' *Friday*, and we are going to the Arts in the Park tomorrow morning. Would anyone like to join us?"

SPEAK "FACE"BOOK?!

"FACE"FRIENDLY

Someone who shows great friendship.

How to use it:

"Hey, buddy! I appreciate how '*F*ace'*friendly* you've been to me lately. I consider you one of my good friends. I hope we can continue this good thing!"

"FACE" FUEL

Something from Facebook that empowers you.

How to use it:

"All these words of encouragement are giving me *'Face'fuel*! I feel like I can finally overcome these obstacles that have been burdening me. Thanks, peeps!"

"FACE"FUZZ

A funny update.

How to use it:

"That's some hysterical '*Face'fuzz*! How in the world did you find yourself in that situation? You better not leave your house next time!"

"FACE"GAIN

When you increase your number of friends.

How to use it:

"Today was a pretty sweet day. I had a 'F*ace'gain* of fourteen friends! I got in contact with a lot of friends from my college days."

SPEAK "FACE"BOOK?!

"FACE"GALS

A group of your female friends on Facebook or all your female friends on Facebook.

How to use it:

"Calling all '*Face'gals*! My good friend just started a clothing business downtown next to the coffee shop. Please go check it out! She has a great variety of items to choose from!"

"FACE" GARAGE

That place where you store all your favorite pictures, videos, articles, and etc. from Facebook.

How to use it:

"That was such a powerful story that I will have to put that in my *'Face'garage*! I will enjoy reading that again and again!"

SPEAK "FACE"BOOK?!

"FACE"GIG

A way to promote your event.

How to use it:

"If you are looking for something to do this Friday night, I have a *'Face'gig* downtown on the square. My band will be playing a two-hour set. Come on out!"

"FACE"GLITCH

A problem.

How to use it:

"Had a '*Face'glitch* this evening. I was having trouble loading a new profile pic and found out my device was the issue. All good now!"

SPEAK "FACE"BOOK?!

"FACE"GLITZ

Being a bit glamorous with your picture and/or posts.

How to use it:

"Nice '*Face'glitz* with that photo from your night out! Looked like everyone was dressed to the T!"

"FACE"GOLD

A very meaningful friend or post.

How to use it:

"Brenna, your recent post was '*Face'gold*! I will treasure the wisdom that was put forth in what you wrote!"

SPEAK "FACE"BOOK?!

"FACE"GUACED

Not guacamole but you did get tricked.

How to use it:

"Man, I thought you were for real in that update. I totally got '*Face'guaced*! I am so gullible!"

"FACE"GUARD

Not becoming friends with everyone who requests it.

How to use it:

"I do some '*Face'guarding* every once in a while—not sure I want to get updates on everyone whom I meet."

SPEAK "FACE"BOOK?!

"FACE"HELP

Assistance with anything and everything.

How to use it:

"*Face'help* needed! I am looking for a plumber whom I can trust. Anybody have one they would recommend?"

"FACE"HOG

A friend who seems to be taking up way too much of your News Feed.

How to use it:

"I barely get a chance to catch up on all my friends' posts because someone (to remain anonymous) is a 'F*ace'hog*! I don't need an update on your update all the time!"

SPEAK "FACE"BOOK?!

"FACE"HONK

A good friend who is a bit loud with their posts.

How to use it:

"Yeah you are a *'Face'honk*, but I do appreciate that you write about how you actually feel."

"FACE" HONKER

A person who draws too much attention to themselves.

How to use it:

"Candice, stop being such a *'Face'honker*! Girl, we don't need a play-by-play of you getting ready every morning!"

"FACE"HOOK

Grabs your attention.

How to use it:

"Once I started reading your post, I was '*Face'hooked*! I hope that you keep that going!"

"FACE"HOUND

Someone who tries to be friends with as many people as possible—could be positive or negative.

How to use it:

"My brother has so many friends on Facebook that he is turning into a *'Face'hound*! I doubt he even really knows half of them."

"FACE"HUG

A fun and meaningful written embrace.

How to use it:

"Congrats on your recent marriage. *'Face'hugs* to you both! Can't wait to see more pictures from your special day!"

"FACE"IAL

A new profile picture.

How to use it:

"Greetings, family and friends! Check out my *'Face'ial*! Took the pic at my niece's wedding!"

"FACE"IDLE

A way to say you will not or have not been using Facebook for a while.

How to use it:

"I have been '*Face'idle* this week. Just have had no time between work, school, and family stuff, so it's been good to catch up with you all!"

"FACE" J–P

ROB KEY

"FACE"JAM

A "selfie" with more than one person in it all crammed together.

How to use it:

"On the elevator going up to the sky suites we took this lovely *'Face'jam*. Everyone was so pumped to see the view!"

SPEAK "FACE"BOOK?!

"FACE"JINGLE

A highly recommended song.

How to use it:

"Got a new *'Face'jingle* for you all to check out. Follow the link to download it."

ROB KEY

"FACE" JUNK

All that stuff you do not want to read.

How to use it:

"Most of the stuff on my News Feed is great, but there is some '*Face'junk* that I would like to get rid of! Guess I should check my settings."

SPEAK "FACE"BOOK?!

"FACE"KABOB

Having more than one picture in your profile picture or other post. A collage.

How to use it:

"Cool *'Face'kabob* of your events today! Looked like the kids were having a blast at the science fair and at the party!"

"FACE"KICK

A good laugh.

How to use it:

"Wow, did I ever get a good '*Face'kick* from your post! That was freaking hilarious!"

"FACE"LAND

When you log into Facebook you enter it.

How to use it:

"It's so good to be back in *'Face'land*! I missed hearing about all your life happenings. I was only offline for three days, but I feel like I missed out on a lot."

"FACE"LESS

Someone who has no profile picture.

How to use it:

"Dude, get a profile pic put up so we can all see the latest and greatest you. Sick of seeing you *'Face'less!*"

"FACE"LIFT

To be encouraged by someone's comment on your Facebook page or to give encouragement to someone by giving a positive comment on their update or wall.

How to use it:

"Thanks for the '*Face'lift* today everyone! Your birthday wishes are much appreciated!"

"FACE"LOVE

A deep appreciation and devotion to your friend(s).

How to use it:

"Much *Face'love* to everyone! You all are so encouraging to me! I am so thankful for each one of you! If there is anything I can do for you, just ask."

SPEAK "FACE"BOOK?!

"FACE"MAGNET

A person who is able to attract a lot of friends to their social networking site.

How to use it:

"My friend Samantha is a *'Face'magnet*! She has so many friends that I can't keep up with her. Everyone she meets requests to be friends with her!"

"FACE" MAKING

Just like it sounds. It could be happy, sad, angry, or you name it.

How to use it:

"Sounds like you had some serious '*Face*'making going on from that post! Yeah, that would have freaked me out as well!"

"FACE"MAN

Facebook superhero.

How to use it:

"Bro, you are '*Face'man*! You are rocking it on Facebook today. So many good thoughts on that issue!"

"FACE" MASK

Someone who is hiding something.

How to use it:

"I know I've been pretty surfacy lately and was *'Face'masking*, but I just needed some time to figure out what I was going to do. So...I ended up taking the job in Dallas!"

SPEAK "FACE"BOOK?!

"FACE"MISSING

A way to help find someone or something that is missing.

How to use it:

"*Face'missing*! *Face'missing*! Has anybody seen my blue purse with the gold bow? I left it at the party yesterday. Please PM me if you find it."

"FACE" MOB

Your friends.

How to use it:

"So, *Face'mob*, anyone feel like meeting up at the movies tonight? I would love to see the one that just came out!"

"FACE"NEST

A safe place to express yourself.

How to use it:

"I want to say a big thank you to all my friends out there! You all have given me a *'Face'nest* where I feel loved and encouraged."

"FACE"NOTIZED

A somewhat hypnotized state where you are on Facebook all the time.

How to use it:

"I never thought I could get addicted to Facebook, but it appears at times I get *'Face'notized*. I have seen others get so enthralled in it that I never pictured myself being the same. I guess it happens to the best of us if we don't pay attention."

SPEAK "FACE"BOOK?!

"FACE"OFF

Will not be using Facebook for a certain period of time.

How to use it:

"I want to let you all know that I'm going '*Face'off* for the next week. I need to get focused on my studies to get my grades up. See you next Monday!"

"FACE" ON

Back on Facebook after a leave of absence.

How to use it:

"I'm '*Face'on* again! It's been a great week of getting caught up with my school work. Feel like I can finish the semester strong now!"

SPEAK "FACE"BOOK?!

"FACE"PAG

Being passive aggressive in your posts.

How to use it:

"What's up with being a *'Face'PAGGER* all of a sudden? Just tell us what you really want. We can help you out, bro!"

ROB KEY

"FACE"PAINT

A picture that is altered with color and graphics.

How to use it:

"I tried out this new app with this photo, and I thought I would share it with everyone. What do you think of this *'Face'paint* creation?"

"FACE"PEAK

Prime hours for Facebooking.

How to use it:

"It appears the hours between 6:00–9:00 p.m. is '*Face'peak* time for my friends…at least that's when I find time to update and read posts."

"FACE"PETS

For all the pet lovers.

How to use it:

"Take a look at my '*Face'pets*! We just got back from the doggie salon, and yes, they have their swagger on!"

SPEAK "FACE"BOOK?!

"FACE"PIGGY

When you share someone's post.

How to use it:

"Hey, folks, I need to *Face'piggy* this! You will be amazed at what this guy can do!"

"FACE"PLANT

Happens when you posted something stupid on Facebook.

How to use it:

"Wow, did I ever just do a *'Face'plant* with that last update! I guess I wasn't thinking straight and posted without reading the whole thing first."

"FACE"PLUG

Putting the word out for something.

How to use it:

"Got a *Face'plug* for my peeps! Go get your hair done at my friend's new salon this week and get half off all services. This girl rocks it!"

"FACE"POINT

A strong argument for or against something.

How to use it:

"Yep, you made a good *'Face'point* with your post. I totally agree with you and hope some changes will begin."

SPEAK "FACE"BOOK?!

"FACE"PONG

It's when you keep commenting/debating back and forth with a particular friend.

How to use it:

"Man, this game of *'Face'pong* we're playing is getting interesting. Others are starting to take notice. But, really now, I am right!"

"FACE"POP

When a friend stops using Facebook.

How to use it:

"Well, I just had a *'Face'pop*. One of my friends decided they were going to stop using Facebook. Hopefully they'll change their minds so I can keep in better contact."

"FACE"POSER

When someone strikes a high school senior picture pose.

How to use it:

"You have got to be kidding me, dude! That's a *'Face'poser* if I've ever seen one. Hilarious!"

"FACE" POSTERED

A picture that shows you getting the better of someone.

How to use it:

"Just *'Face'postered* my friend. He had no clue I was coming around the corner!"

SPEAK "FACE"BOOK?!

"FACE"POSSE

A group of very close friends.

How to use it:

"Thanks again to my '*Face'posse*! You guys were tremendous with your help on that project. What would I have done without you?"

"FACE"PRO

One who updates frequently.

How to use it:

"I must say that I'm turning into a '*Face'pro*! Been on the ball with my posts lately and feel like my peeps know what's going on with me."

SPEAK "FACE"BOOK?!

"FACE"PROOF

A post or picture that is safe to put on Facebook.

How to use it:

"Sometimes I feel like posting stuff about whatever is going on in my family's life, but then I stop myself to make sure it is *'Face'proof*. Gotta protect the fam!"

ROB KEY

"FACE" PUNCH

A friendly jab at you or at a friend's post on Facebook.

How to use it:

"Yes, I got a lot of *'Face'punches* about my last status update, but they were all well deserved on my part!"

"FACE"PUSH

Trying to get more friends.

How to use it:

"Today I made a concerted effort to find more friends on Facebook. The '*Face'push* paid off as I hooked up with about a dozen more!"

"FACE" Q–S

"FACE"Q

Your Facebook intelligence.

How to use it:

"Jose, you have such a high *'Face'Q*. Your use of Facebook shows great thinking and integrity!"

SPEAK "FACE"BOOK?!

"FACE"RACE

A race with friends where you check in at various points.

How to use it:

"I'm super geeked about the *'Face'race* today! Starting at Moe's and making our way to Robert's Diner. Game on, friends!"

"FACE"RAMBLE

Saying really nothing in your post just because you felt like it.

How to use it:

"I know that I was *'Face'rambling* yesterday, but I just wanted to type whatever came to mind. It was rather random I must say!"

SPEAK "FACE"BOOK?!

"FACE"RANK

How you rank your friends. Those who are close versus those who are casual.

How to use it:

"Bryan, you are in the upper tier of my friends according to how I '*Face'rank*. So just know that you are truly valued!"

"FACE"RATE

How you rate a photo, whether it's a winner or a loser.

How to use it:

"Alright, guys! Give me a '*Face'rate* on this new photo. Please give me your honest opinion. Thanks so much!"

SPEAK "FACE"BOOK?!

"FACE"READ

An interesting article, blog, etc.

How to use it:

"Here's a *'Face'read* that I would highly recommend! So many great thoughts on how to stay at your peak health."

"FACE" RUNNERS

A running club of friends.

How to use it:

"*Face'runners*, lets hook up for a five miler before work tomorrow. We can meet at my place. My wife will have breakfast smoothies ready for us afterward!"

"FACE"SALE

Selling something on Facebook.

How to use it:

"I have decided to do a '*Face'sale*. Going to sell my SUV. Check out the picture, and private message me if you are interested. Thanks!"

"FACE"SAVER

One that saves people's pictures from Facebook.

How to use it:

"Chuck, you take such great pictures that I end up saving most of them. The '*Face'saver* in me just needs to see them more than once!"

"FACE"SHACKLES

One has them on when they do not show their true selves on Facebook.

How to use it:

"Girl, get rid of those '*Face'shackles*! You need to just be who you are to the world. Don't worry about what people think about you so much."

"FACE"SHIELD

Something you use to protect yourself or the act of protecting yourself.

How to use it:

"Lately, I have been keeping my *Face'shield* up. Don't want to give away my whereabouts at every moment of every day."

SPEAK "FACE"BOOK?!

"FACE"SHIFT

Changing your thought on something you previously posted.

How to use it:

"Made a major '*Face'shift* today. I admit I was too quick to judge. Feel better about my approach now."

"FACE"SHINED

The act of cleaning up your Facebook homepage.

How to use it:

"Updated my homepage today. It was definitely in need of a '*Face'shine*!"

"FACE"SHOP

Looking for new friends.

How to use it:

"Enjoyed doing some '*Face*'*shopping* this afternoon. Was so glad to find so many grade school classmates on Facebook!"

"FACE"SHOT

Taking jabs at a post or picture.

How to use it:

"Good grief, I took a lot of '*Face'shots* from that update. I thought it was funny, but apparently it crossed the line a little. Sorry, folks!"

SPEAK "FACE"BOOK?!

"FACE"SHOUT

A big affirmation of a friend.

How to use it:

"Here's a '*Face'shout* to my homey Wesley! You played like a man on fire in tonight's game! You lit them up from three point range!"

"FACE"SICK

Missed using Facebook.

How to use it:

"Felt '*Face'sick* today even though I was only off Facebook for a couple of days. I'm not addicted to it, but I do miss seeing your updates."

"FACE"SIGHTING

Sightings of well-known people.

How to use it:

"I didn't expect to have this *'Face'sighting* at breakfast, but the mayor came in and sat at the table right next to ours. I guess he likes a good omelet to start the day like I do!"

"FACE"SKID

When your post leaves a bad impression.

How to use it:

"Hey, sis. I don't think that message came across like you wanted it to. It certainly left a '*Face'skid*. Might want to think twice before you post next time."

"FACE"SKIP

When you bypass a potential friend.

How to use it:

"Am I a goon when I '*Face'skip* some friends? There are a few people out there I would rather avoid than to be in everyday contact with."

ROB KEY

"FACE"SKIZZY

A warm and fuzzy status update or comment.

How to use it:

"What a great '*Face'skizzy*! You really know how to make me feel good!"

SPEAK "FACE"BOOK?!

"FACE"SLAMMED

When your news feed is crazy busy.

How to use it:

"Does everyone have good news or what today? My feed is *Face'slammed* with all kinds of great stuff!"

"FACE"SLASHER

Someone who interjects well into a conversation in the comment area.

How to use it:

"Paul, my friend, you have earned the title of *Face'slasher*! You have intriguing thoughts that keep everyone interested and active in my posts."

"FACE"SMOG

The unwanted stuff on your News Feed.

How to use it:

"Had to bypass a lot of '*Face'smog* tonight. I only got to catch up on only about half the updates. What's up with that?"

"FACE"SNUBBED

Being rejected from being a friend with someone.

How to use it:

"I think I was just *Face'snubbed* by my friend from nursing school…guess she didn't value our friendship as much as I did."

"FACE"SOLVER

One that figures out a potential friend's identity.

How to use it:

"I needed quite a few clues, but I finally figured out which Mr. Lee was the right one from the big city. My *'Face'solver* instincts took over!"

ROB KEY

"FACE"SPECTIVE

Your current perspective.

How to use it:

"My *Face'spective* today after lunch… taking in this band who was playing in the plaza…so beautiful!"

SPEAK "FACE"BOOK?!

"FACE"SPEED

It is how fast you comment or like someone's update.

How to use it:

"As soon as I read someone's update, I like to comment as quickly as possible so they can act on my feedback if needed. Swift '*Face'speed* can really help out a brother in need!"

"FACE" SPICE

Flavorful updates or comments.

How to use it:

"Ben, that was some incredible '*Face'spice* in your post! The thought you put into it was over-the-top!"

"FACE"SPIN

It is how you give a topic your own thought.

How to use it:

"Your '*Face'spin* on that subject was stellar! Big props to you, my friend!"

ROB KEY

"FACE"SPIRATION

Inspirational quotes.

How to use it:

"Have you had your *Face'spiration* today? If not, give this a read! Time well spent!"

SPEAK "FACE"BOOK?!

"FACE"SPLASH

An update that gets lots of likes and comments.

How to use it:

"For some reason, the posts that I think are worth reading don't get much attention while my so-called weaker posts (in my eyes) make a bigger *'Face'splash*. Go figure!"

"FACE" STAR

Someone who is very popular on your Facebook.

How to use it:

"My cousin Ryan is a '*Face'star*! He gets more likes on his posts than any other of my friends. He is so well received!"

SPEAK "FACE"BOOK?!

"FACE"STREET

The News Feed.

How to use it:

"I was strolling down '*Face'street* today and was surprised to see that my former teammate from college moved back to town! That's totally nectar!"

"FACE" STUDY

An opinion poll of your friends.

How to use it:

"Hey, everyone! I am doing a *'Face'study* and would like to know what you think of the new product line that I am selling. Please be honest with me. I value your feedback!"

"FACE"STYLE

The classy way to post your words and pictures.

How to use it:

"Jayden, you have an impressive *Face'style*! Your news is always so well put together, and your pictures just speak for themselves!"

"FACE" SWABS

Useful ideas to clean up your posts or pictures.

How to use it:

"I should have put a *'Face'swab* to use before I posted that picture. Should have brightened it so you could actually see my wife's facial expression. Maybe I'm staying out of trouble this way!"

"FACE"SWOP

Changing a profile picture.

How to use it:

"Did a '*Face'swop* again. I wasn't too pleased with my hair that day in my previous photo. Having a better hair day today!"

"FACE"SYNC

When you post regular updates.

How to use it:

"Mom, you've been in great '*Face'sync* all this week! Love it when I know what's going on with you!"

"FACE" T–Z

"FACE"TAG

Like phone tag except on Facebook.

How to use it:

"I keep trying to connect with you in real time on Facebook but to no avail, so *'Face'tag*, you're it!"

"FACE"TAN

It's what you get when you are on Facebook frequently.

How to use it:

"Oh my, your '*Face'tan* is showing up big time! You are online all flipping day!"

"FACE"TARDY

It's when you are late to comment on someone's post.

How to use it:

"Sorry for being '*Face'tardy*. I'm sure your concert went fantastic. Wish I had read about it sooner, but thanks so much for the invite!"

SPEAK "FACE"BOOK?!

"FACE"TEMP

Measured by how often you post something.

How to use it:

"My *Face'temp* has been running high lately. Been posting probably too many pics, and I sense they are showing up as a fever. Don't want to get on anyone's nerves."

"FACE"TIPS

Pieces of advice or expert information.

How to use it:

"*Face'tips* needed! I need help with fixing my computer. It is slower than a teenager getting out of bed on a Saturday morning!"

SPEAK "FACE"BOOK?!

"FACE"TOWELS

Useful ideas to help clean up your homepage.

How to use it:

"I need one good wipe with a *'Face'towel* to make my homepage look better. It just looks grimy!"

"FACE" TRAFFIC

Measured by how busy your News Feed is.

How to use it:

"I cannot believe all the *'Face'traffic* tonight! Lots of life-changing events are happening as I write this. Very solid night!"

SPEAK "FACE"BOOK?!

"FACE"TRAVEL

Getting from point A to point B. Travel and points of interest ideas.

How to use it:

"Anyone know the best way to get around the construction zone on Main Street? Need some *'Face'travel* help! Also, any good ice cream shops in the area while I'm up there?"

"FACE"UP

Thumbs-up. Like.

How to use it:

"*Face'up* on that, Brad! That idea is beyond anything I could have come up with on my own."

"FACE"VALUE

A positive way to acknowledge someone.

How to use it:

"Dad, you have outstanding '*Face'value*! Your love and words of wisdom are immeasurable. Thanks for always being there (online) even though we are far apart. Blessings!"

"FACE"VIEW

Your opinion.

How to use it:

"My *'Face'view* is that the team should practice one additional time a week so that the chemistry among the players is at a high level."

SPEAK "FACE"BOOK?!

"FACE"VITE

Using the social network to invite your friends to an event.

How to use it:

"Hey, everyone! Here's your special 'F*ace'vite* to my sister's baby shower. Save the date and time. Other details to come soon. You don't want to miss it!"

"FACE"VOGUE

Very stylish posts.

How to use it:

"Madam, that was 'F*ace*'*vogue* at its finest! So lovely and thought provoking—a thing of beauty!"

"FACE"WALKERS

A walking group of friends.

How to use it:

"Okay, *'Face'walkers*, let's try to do the Walk for a Cure next month. If you can make it, let me know, and I will get you the registration info."

"FACE"WALLY

The game of "Where am I?" using pictures and clues.

How to use it:

"*'Face'Wally* time! Can anyone guess where I am sitting right now? It's hard to believe that I even had access to this place."

SPEAK "FACE"BOOK?!

"FACE"WAR

The states, provinces, territories, and countries you have conquered because you have friends in them.

How to use it:

"Hey there, everyone! I'm up to twenty-seven states and five countries in *'Face'war*. How about anyone else?"

"FACE" WASH

Getting your posts and pictures cleaned up.

How to use it:

"Another *'Face'wash* done today. Out with some old pictures and in with some new ones. Feels good to update my page."

"FACE"WISH

It's the friend you have not found yet.

How to use it:

"I have this '*Face'wish* who I have been looking for since I got on Facebook. Hopefully sooner or later she will join Facebook so we can unite again."

"FACE"WORK

Doing Facebook stuff.

How to use it:

"Got some *'Face'work* done today. No, not a nose job! But I did post some pictures from our vacation in Maui. Hope you all enjoy them!"

"FACE"WRECKED

When you cannot get to Facebook because of computer (or any other technical) issues.

How to use it:

"I was *'Face'wrecked* all day yesterday because my cell phone was on the blink. Finally figured out the problem, so now I'm back to normalcy."

"FACE"WRINKLE

A post that shows how old you are getting.

How to use it:

"James, you are showing signs of a *'Face'wrinkle* with your update. 'Going to bed at ten on a Friday night?' Back in the day, you were just getting started then!"

"FACE"YOKED

An extremely strong or powerful update, picture, or comment.

How to use it:

"Man, that picture is *'Face'yoked*! You really motivated me to begin that fitness plan! I have been procrastinating for years."

"FACE"ZIT

Small imperfection(s) with a post.

How to use it:

"Yes, I know I have some spelling errors in that post, so excuse my *'Face'zits*. I was in a flurry and had to get you all updated."

SPEAK "FACE"BOOK?!

"FACE"ZOMBIE

One who is on Facebook but never uses it.

How to use it:

"Anyone out there have some *'Face'zombies*? I have about a dozen of them. It would be great to hear from them instead of this nothingness. Come on, people!"

CPSIA information can be obtained at www.ICGtesting.com
Printed in the USA
LVOW04s1508020615

440867LV00014B/483/P